To Lino

From

Thali
Teagan

Paul & Mary
xo love
+see you Soon
xo.

Let there be Love

Panographs® by Ken Duncan

Introduction

What is Love? One of the most commonly used words in the English language - but possibly the most misunderstood. I have asked many people, "What is love?", and been astounded at some of the answers. No wonder people have difficulties in loving when there is little understanding of what true love is. Through the following pages I would like to share with you the most profound description of true love that I have ever encountered. As you enjoy the beauty of God's creation in these photographs, I hope the accompanying words enrich your understanding of what love really is.

Ken Duncan.

Love is $\mathcal{K}$ind

Love is $\mathcal{P}$atient

Love is
never *Jealous*

Love is
never $\mathscr{B}$oastful

Love is
never $\mathcal{P}$roud

Love is
never *R*ude

Love isn't *S*elfish

Love isn't
*Q*uick tempered

Love doesn't keep
a record of *W*rongs
that others do

Love rejoices in
the *Truth*

Love doesn't rejoice
in *E*vil

Love is always *Supportive*

Love is always *Loyal*

Love is always
Hopeful

Love is always
Trusting

Love never *Fails!*

*W*hat if I could speak all languages of humans and of angels?

If I did not love others, I would be nothing more than a noisy gong or a clanging cymbal.

What if I could prophesy and understand all secrets and all knowledge?

And what if I had faith that moved mountains?

I would be nothing, unless I loved others.

What if I gave away all that I owned and let myself be burnt alive?

    I would gain nothing, unless I loved others.

*L*ove is kind and patient, never jealous, boastful, proud, or rude.

Love isn't selfish or quick tempered. It doesn't keep a record of wrongs that others do.

Love rejoices in the truth, but not in evil.

Love is always supportive, loyal, hopeful, and trusting.

    Love never fails!

1 Corinthians Chapter 13 verses 1 to 8

PHOTO INDEX

Let There Be Love

FIRST PUBLISHED IN 1996
THIS EDITION PUBLISHED 1997
BY KEN DUNCAN PANOGRAPHS® PTY LTD
ACN 050 235 606
PO BOX 15, WAMBERAL NSW 2260
TELEPHONE: (02) 4367 6777

ISBN 0 9586681 6 7
PHOTOGRAPHY© KEN DUNCAN 1997
CEV TEXT© AMERICAN BIBLE SOCIETY 1995

DISTRIBUTED BY
THE BIBLE SOCIETY IN AUSTRALIA INC.
30 YORK ROAD, INGLEBURN NSW 2565
PRINTED IN HONG KONG BY SOUTH
CHINA PRINTING CO.